TRAVELING WITH COYOTES

Poems & Diary
by

JENNIFER MOYER

SPOON RIVER POETRY PRESS
1987

This book is published in part with funds provided by the Illinois Arts Council, a state organization, and by the National Endowment for the Arts. Our thanks.

Traveling with Coyotes copyright (C) 1987 by Jennifer Moyer. All rights reserved. No portion of this book may be reproduced in any manner without written permission of the author, except for quotations embodied in reviews and articles.

Published by Spoon River Poetry Press, David R. Pichaske, editor; P. O. Box 1443; Peoria, Illinois 61655.

Cover: Lyonel Feininger, "Adventure II," 1940, used by permission of Serge Sabarsky Gallery. Very special thanks to Serge Sabarsky.

Typesetting by Rodine the Printer, Peoria, Illinois.

Printing by Gesme's Printing, Marshall, Minnesota.

ISBN 0-933180-92-6

for Britt

CONTENTS

Preface	2
Number 6	4
It's Omaha	5
Moose Creek Lodge	6
Plum Tart	8
Lighthouse Keeper	9
Fairbanks, Alaska	10
Genoa. Columbus Day 1985	12
No Pasaje	13
Saving Marbles	14
At the Border	17
In Memoriam	18
Coyotes	19
In Francesca's Attic	20
They Are Digging My Grave with a Backhoe	22
The Pattern of Things	23
Hemlocks	24
Milk Hill	25
From the Diary of Anna	26

TRAVELING WITH COYOTES

PREFACE
Somewhere in 1981

We climb the hill to our house
leaving behind a whisper
and silence.

There are brown leaves
that cover my heart sometimes,
reproductions
of the fine lines of trees,
fragile and light.
They escape in the wind,
cover the earth.
Deer walk over
with hooves like pencil points.
A fox turns its eyes at your headlights.

Stars above the trees
are barely audible.
The moon multiplies itself.
You build me a fire,
kneel on the other side of fallen trees
breathing woodpeckers.
The house is the stakes
that mark this air
from the edge of the woods.

We walk up to fox holes
to stare.
Trees bend
in thin arcs.
Ferns are still green,
the wind in a spiral around the weeds.
I keep thinking it was moose
not deer that were snorting
at the edge of the water
with the moon rising, falling
above the hill.

Nights unfold
from the grillwork of days,
in the way that you and I arrive
and move through the evening together,
wind through the white pines.
Always.
As the train runs out of this world
into our own,
waiting for thirty-two years
to live like this.

NUMBER 6

He was nobody, man.
Just like you and me.
Tells us of Jesus on the Lex line
her pants as tight as kneesocks
on Friday, raining,
a February evening.
We give our children
a new disease. It's killing them.
There's some money to be made here.

And in a suburb a preacher,
with platform attendees,
steps to the edge of the curb.
A train rushes out the sound,
the light.

There used to be sheep in the Bronx.
Now we work for trade magazines
and worry when our children come
to visit and we're gone.
Memories of Sunday mornings
the three of us under, on top of the covers
and the dog.

Planes have been running late
for two and one half years.
You can't notice every time.
We switch to the next calamity
from dorm nickname
to the ice that rides over phone wires.
You buddy.
Don't get stuck nowhere.

IT'S OMAHA

When he arrived with no books
he stood, reading newspaper
lining the drawers.
Solitary lisp of pages turning.

Buzz of neon,
a fly's lengthy death
at a corner of the pane.
Regret
makes him restless,
so he moves shoes from suitcase to closet.

Light and smells of coffee shop cooking,
hamburger tasting
slightly like metal grill, the girl
lumpy, bad
teeth and hair, always bristle
and friz, an attack.

Back with his socks,
grit brushed off
only buttons left, two buzzes,
intrusion of recognition
of this place
his face above the soup,
and sheets,
limp and cool dampness
always hits you in the middle of the back.

MOOSE CREEK LODGE
for Debby

So they buy the place.
Six cabins
with beds and a chair.
Where the Yukon and Klondike meet
200 miles outside White Horse.

Selling wolf, bear, beaver skins,
and sour dough rolls
they call it a tea room.
Soundless arc of snow
interrupted by baking smells.

On a summer day
a bear gets into the kitchen
so they shoot it.
Don't know, do you eat bear?
Now the traps are filled
with salmon and pineapple,
sardines for the racoons.

In winter they do the books
and short order cooking.
Loggers, oilman, trappers
play blackjack at Diamond Tooth Gurdy's.
She leaves them smashed.

On long nights
when the sun never sets,
they don't think of New Jersey,
people standing on street corners
like old clothes on hooks.
Backed up rivers with flag poles
on the banks, the picnic tables,
trash and weeds filling up the curb
and the first whiff of honeysuckle
reminding them of childhood.

Don't think of it,
an old girlfriend, a stripper,
now a computer programmer,
children, the slurpees,
careful hairdos,
the way light hits the windows
in the rain.

They sink
into the long low cast
of Northern evenings,
light sifting through the wind,
wooden counters
with lemon meringue pies cooling
before the snows, drifts, the storms,
barrier reefs against the world.

PLUM TART

She hears cars on the wet streets outside.
Awnings drip on their knees.
The hostess says to them in English,
You become fish,
and you become wild deer
and changes their silverware.
In the bath next to the bedroom
there is a hammer on the sink.
They don't ask about it or the screwdrivers.

The train moves them in between
pumpkins getting plump in rows,
sheep and stucco cathedrals.
At dusk all the church bells ring
lighting their way down a muddy path.

They suck the foam off pils,
order plum tarts
sliced into dishes of yellowing cream.
Hikers have spaetzle
and slice into rabbit head.

The bell on the tan lead cow
sounds like wind chimes
in the valley.
She recognizes the lines on the face
of an old woman
pulling a wheelbarrow full of turnips
behind her up a pasture.
The broad flat hips.

Honking geese scatter
in the evening light.
She tucks her scarf in at the neck.
Night backs up.
Their train takes them back
and she hears cars on the wet streets outside,
but it's not raining, it's Paris.

LIGHTHOUSE KEEPER

Leaving with the moon and minus tide
sounds of engine and fog
cover up Mt. Hood.
This morning it's white fish and salt.
Cormorants duck under water for food.
We sweep sand and fish gills
onto the deck, watching the sun
sink into Pearl Island.

The salmon are running.
Not here, he says.
He doesn't hear the fog horn either.
Lingcod get cleaned and fried for dinner—
bottles of wine, wild rhododendrons—
the rest flopping under the deck.

Night air fills with wet
left after a day of rain,
empty skeleton heads,
sounds of deer hooves
on a bed of pine needles.
We buy six pound weights
and beer,
check tide charts, dig for clams
catching their flat corners under wet heavy sand.
In the calmest part
killer whales arc out of the Sound
and in again.

We keep the glove compartment shut
with scotch tape,
drain the last salt water
down a side street.
Fish heads rot in a box.
Clouds are gathering in outskirts.
The children ignore us,
riding their plastic bikes over and over
through pine needles, gutters, and rain.

FAIRBANKS, ALASKA

September, 1954
for Margaret

Dawn is curling at the edges
as we drive a pickup down the dirt road.
Really, we expected something else
but there across from Ft. Wainwright
is the Club Tokyo and the auto dump.

The Reverend Dr. Lloyd Ritter, ex-Marine,
his Japanese bride from World War II
running the place.
The marriage commissioner.
He can sell fishing licenses
and marriages.
We are his thirteenth,

He puts our names in the wrong places
drawing lines to the right ones.
The statutes are pretty thin, he says.
D'ya want anything special?

The Reverend's wife stays in the kitchen
washing dishes.
It takes him eleven seconds or so to marry us.
They are in between the lunch and dinner shifts.

We have one picture,
a streak of light
from a hole in the roof,
background of tables
turned upside down to mop the floor.
It was awful.
It was wonderful.
Giggles escape on our way out the musty door
sitting on the outside steps with a bottle
of Japanese plum wine.
A gift from the Reverend.

Transvestite waiters
at the steak house.
We get drunk,
waiting for three days
while a friend tries to get his boat
started.
We buy some frozen salmon,
and bring home a copy of the marriage certificate
just in case.

GENOA. COLUMBUS DAY 1985

At night it is afternoon.
The needle rests on
Camel Stationary Traveler.
Reagan's hijacking on tv.
She serves stale beer,
sugar, and cognac in a coffee cup.

Noise shuts down at dark.
Men lean shoulders
against concrete,
leftovers stuck in a garbage can too long.

Beds don't budge and
fill up the bedroom.
Thin mismatched sheets
with a tablecloth on top.
Lebanese men next door
watch the bathroom.

Clatter of dogs against the fountain,
ammonia,
cats on the scaffolding.

He holds the fish up by the tail,
fries it with rosemary and garlic,
raw onions and vinegar a specialty.
Next to the window there is
bougainvilla and the Mediterranean.
Or is it oleander.

She bums a light next to a fresco,
the narrow streets deserted.
They sightsee in the dark.

No parade. Only a statue
next to the train station.

NO PASAJE

Borders hiss downhill.
In a tunnel smoke lies softly
on seat cushions and glass.
Wide wales of light
run into a green green sea.

After cheese,
cottonwood and aspen.
Everything planted except for mountains.
Shorn sheep and muts trot
into dust and crumbling towns,
Some are goats. It's hard to tell.

Magpies hop along rocks,
dry whistle of hawks.
They come out of beads
for glances and chatter,
desolation, red earth.
A tire breaks off the road into dirt.
No pasaje.

A widow in black spreads out
over weep holes in a low rock wall,
ancient olive trees in rows to the sunset.
Cattle creak.
 Standing with a beer,
boot heel on a brass rail,
mirage of night and tameness,
rituals of certainty and time.

SAVING MARBLES

There are careful routes here
to take with the wet leaves,
a ridge at the edge of morning.
My hands steam and are impatient
with the angle of light and intent.

Someone is vacuuming outside my door.
I wait for the hum and scream
to bump back down the steps
before I turn the rust off the knob
and step out into the day.
There is a pattern they call nutmeg
an oblique shadow
on my shoe and gloves.

With the turn of this edge
and that hallway
white porcelain slips
from my view and the cool
rush of the cat
stops the dizziness.

I stick to the shadow
and the breeze
throwing bicyclists off their paths
sails tipping
to loons and murk
at the place where the lagoon
and overpass meet.

The sun stays quiet today
and moves in its solid way
across my forehead,
peeling cold skin
from a sour green apple.

There are striped yellow umbrellas
and women in white sip
on straws of iced tea,
flaunting lunches
and inflections.
Their thoughts escape in wisps,
evaporating.

If I open the box
there is a purple tint
to the green stems
and red in the creaks of the floor boards.
This paint covers the sound of footsteps
following maps of years
halting
and getting started again.

The cat bumps his head
against the listlessness.
Squeeze its bones
and long nipples
between the lines on my fingers.
Erase this crease.

The porch screen
cages sounds
running up and down
the center of the house
like an elevator.

The horses have not passed by here
three times today.
Just some false hope,
women in clogs going uphill
or down.
Faint stirring of moss
and geranium
in between the brick walk.

I hold a long ray of waxy light
from the bottom of the milk carton
the cool and weight
holding down my papers
and the urge to sink for good
into plastic strips
of a lawn chair.

There are silhouettes of books,
suggestions of Mahler
and conversation
when summer folds itself around
the corner
and the screen door slams shut.
I rush to get the balls off
in the right direction
their colors rolling over.

The slats are the deck.
Pebbles and tar stare at the cracks.
Dirty feet flap at chairs
and other prerequisites.
Some of us will save the marbles
and chocolate covered almonds,
melting
from the nostrils
of our children.

AT THE BORDER

Kansas, 1958.
Cows hump over the water trough,
baby hawk feathers
ruffle in the wind and dust
balancing on the wire fence.

Mylo is turning brown.
Your tongue sticks
to the roof of your mouth
it's so dry.

Climbing 4,000 feet in 400 miles
gullies dry up,
the wheat topped and stored,
fields burned up to the fence posts.

Sunflowers and millet
crowd in a lump
at the edge of the weeds
where the swallows go.

Grasses browned
to a purple tinge
the grey and the roan
nose to pink nose.
Impossible to imagine
fetlocks in snow.

IN MEMORIAM

Rhododendrons hide her face
and head, neat spreading
of napkin, the bag,
half sandwich and apple,
the thermos. It smells of coffee
as she pours out lemonade
and sets the cup in the sun.
Gnats hover.
An airplane overhead,
35 seconds after, 36 now
and she closes the book,
the sun hitting her knees
making them flushed and hot.

Trees don't move,
water and time hiss through pipes
with a catch.
Slowly the clock tower blocks the sun.
The wooden bench is in memoriam,
carved Gothic letters that wear
and go gray.

Clover in the grass clippings,
and name of the English teacher's son,
somewhere on a black slate memorial.
They wash it by hand from buckets.
Children slide their fingers
over the letters,
the names.
Some from here,
some from there.
Still adding names.

COYOTES

The sky reminds her
of Shidoni,
above the Piñyon
black volcanic rock,
drinking Tequila and lemon,
10 in the morning at the hot springs,
smell of sage, anvil clouds,
squaw grass,
clear frigid water
from the mountains,
a grandmother
born in New Mexico before it was a state.
And the waitress, *Someone
has been here a long time.*
She says, *I hope I'm here
when you get here.*
They travel fast to Tesuque
and Española.
No river now, just the pine trees
and wind sluicing between rocks,
view of 11,000 square miles,
temperature dropping
from 90 to 62
climbing to the top.

No one camps near them.
They roast ears of corn—
advice from an uncle
to his grandson, *Eat it
like a typewriter.*
The sun sliding behind
the mountain and stormfront.
Listen once as coyotes
call out above them
as if they hadn't been there,
as if they weren't.

IN FRANCESCA'S ATTIC

The same galvanized barn
and cats, a sneaking streak
down or up the steps.
Piglets squealing hilarity
around corners spying us
from one side then the other.
The mut runs madly barking
to keep them penned.

At the dinner table
we spread desire around
like napkins, the trim
painted a fresh eggshell
and Francesca,
When the fire gets started,
the top goes down.

Transported,
pale light falling
from pink and ruffled lampshades,
an adolescent bedroom with secrets
stuffed under the bed.
Dust and make-believe
on a Saturday afternoon
when winter sun
shows up grubby baseboards.
You notice trees
out the second story window,
like glasses on passersby
but the coat is what stands out
the way they hunch inside.

When the fire gets started,
you play the boy and
I'll play the girl.
We make up the rest
since the last she'd heard
from a boy he'd said,
You look like you've been hit

by a semi and she buys B-cup
bras from then on.
She asks her father what a semi is.

Light that seems benevolent
diffused through thin patterned curtains
rests on top of the bureau
painted a powder blue.
The rug unraveling at one edge,
metal bedframe
barking the shins of her mother.

The door closed,
the room a castle,
stables for our horses and tack,
tea in the garden
high curved brick walls,
close-cropped lawns, roses,
dialogue that we make up
as we go along.

A servant refills our cups,
we discipline the children,
languish over longing,
nostalgia spilling
like our arms, draped over
white metal lawn chairs,
wisteria perfuming the place,
and we are enraptured, captured.

THEY ARE DIGGING MY GRAVE WITH A BACKHOE

They are digging my grave with a backhoe,
a hurricane off the Florida coast,
and snow predicted for today is rain.
In the movies faces are prettier.
You go on tending your own,
ruts frozen in the road.

A light through junk birches;
only my sister cries.
He starts to write
I need some minor thing . . .
and the preacher quits after a minute or so.
Pallbearers in their greasy coats
kick at mosquitos down the hill,
and they can't match the typeface
on the stone.
But somebody mows.
It's not the grave that bothers me
but the diggers.

And on the way back
brilliant October coloring
diffuses the green.
A batch of children playing,
their squeals, the leaves
about to fall, falling,
and the sky a bright, bright blue
before the song comes on.

THE PATTERN OF THINGS
>   *for John Kelly*

The color of lawn fades to pee,
a few brush strokes for pines,
trees the color of smoke stacks.
He has the smell
of an old fashioned wrist watch.

Wool itches his thighs.
He talks about Chinese fried slugs
we had at dinner at breakfast. She
about restrictions on bringing
Cuban lovers into town.
It's Christmas for Christ's sake
and no lover in sight.
Not a car in Star Market's parking lot.

The dog slips across the ice.
We follow No Trespassing signs
through wind and cold that make us
fierce mortals.
Gloves muffle the hand's path.
Vision sharp as the crisp edge
of a fallen leaf.

Later, the fire makes us sleepy,
dipping our lips in hot toddies
mouthing cool jazz.
She catches cold,
hoarse,
her first patient deaf.
Sure still beats drinking scotch
in a fleabag hotel in Paris
with a Sony Walkman on.

HEMLOCKS

The day unrolling
like a bolt of cloth.
Piano notes rush and fall staccato
spilling out over the edge
of the window and the window ledge.

Sun slants from cheekbone
to a corner of our serenity.
Daffodils nod
over their pale places
on the table of china and lace.

We peel back cuffs and prop ankles
on white spring chairs
fresh from seven weeks of rain.
A cool drink drips on our thighs.
Tulips bunch their red petals high

turning black pistils
to the west
as light and sound
are squeezed from the tops
of the scattered hemlocks.

Two bats twirl in the murky air
and the sun drops
like the eye along a gable,
the latch
of a door closing, catches.

MILK HILL

Basil has Tanya draw an onion
and milk bottle.
She paints a yellow square,
the March sky
and smell of bedrooms
warm and stuffy,
lighting the first cigarette of the day.

Too early for tea
we drink malt whiskey,
suck on dry Cuban cigars.
The publican in the next stone house
stays home with his sheep,
swans lying in the green field
with the lambs,
black bracken
and tips of heather blooming
in whites and pinks.

Scrap metal and horses graze
out one side of the train,
the woman with our coffee
comes down the aisles
and I can't remember whether
there are now more people dead than alive
or is it more people alive than dead?

Tanya goes home
and Basil dies in the hospital.
We get plastic refills for the coffee,
smoking cigarettes, the businessmen
read their memos,
and the train, 90 miles per hour,
streams past a man in his Wellingtons
holding a boy and a girl by each hand,
in rapt attention, fields green and wet,
one brilliant ray of April sun
after all the rain
falls on the wool of his jacket.
And from where I sit, no one else can see it.

FROM THE DIARY OF ANNA

June 30

I hear whispers like cross bars in the bridge. We swim off the rocks to the old train trestle. The sun is going down; swimming into the middle of the lake blocks all ordinary sounds, stress, telephone conversations. My companion is the rhythm of my breath.

July 3

Taking a parkway up to the Adirondacks, we climb to the top of the highest peak, stand in pools of rain on the rock. Wind blows the clouds through us. Handholds in the rock drip; we climb down, digging our heels into the face, 3,000 feet to the bottom rock-filled streambed. The clouds lift and cover the sun.

We build a fire and grill open-faced cheese sandwiches, drink hot coffee and cognac. At night, inside the tent, I hear my breath next to the wind, like standing on tiptoes.

July 4

We dip water out of a pool on the rock and make cocoa and apricot biscuits over the coals. The same birds are calling. Climbing down we hold onto tree roots and look out when the clouds push back. We are taller than the trees. There is a rhythm to climbing up and down the mountains; we find it on the third day.

The trail hovers at the edge of Avalanche Lake, running underneath the rock. Two climbers scale a rock face. We take off our clothes and dive into the cold. Later we drink from the lake. A song bird sings us lunch and the sun comes out for a few minutes. Two hikers walk off the trail to watch us swim. Cold? they ask. We see them look back farther around the lake. The climbers lift themselves out of view, their orange pack under the trees. Voices echo against rock walls that surface and rise up. We rub the chill out of our skin with the wrong side of a towel and lean back against the rocks.

We have scrambled omelet, biscuits and honey for dinner. We read to each other over the fire and let the coals flicker and undulate like seaweed. There are no stars.

July 7

Watch today. It's oppressive so New York stays outside. I take the corner to St. Mark's Place slowly to avoid the heat. One man hisses. A cab follows a truck like a starling after a crow, beating at its tale. I am ordinary, invisible. The natives stand out; an old woman, somebody's mother, in a housecoat and slippers shuffling across the street, like her front yard. A kid stands next to the curb watching two beds on a dolly. He yells up to his girlfriend. Hey. We should get these for our apartment. She answers, what apartment? A fly is the only occupant of the tables next door, sitting on the salt shaker. A man with a Van Husen eye patch walks by. He looks embarassed. The boy answers, when we get an apartment.

We are sunk like heat on the steps in the middle of Manhattan. Drinking ale at McSorley's we knock down a man's crutches. We buy poori, sweet lassi and beer from the deli.

Walking back from 53rd Street I get a headache, losing it lying on top of the sheets.

July 8

I think, what am I doing here? I can't remember where I was. I am standing in the Laundromat facing the breeze. That helps. It is in the 90's today and the top of the lake is warm to swim through. At the Belmore I think through all the ways to cheat on the meal ticket. There are old women here and old men, cab drivers. Suddenly it's New York in my lunches, New York in my sleep.

Two boys stand on the trestle and ask how far I'm swimming, how far I've come. A paper cup floats on the water and breaks my pace.

At the hair dresser's, the sweeper calls Salvatore a fucker

and a coke freak. He hasn't been paid. He yells into the walls of gray carpet. Clients are scattered around like fashion magazines.

Heat moves along the railroad tracks like a slow train.

July 15

It was cool and windy last night, blowing the noises from the street in my window every hour or so. Empty flatbeds and semis bump over the pot holes and layers of street. Once I wake up to total silence.

Two Guatemalen knife throwers ask for Christmas beer in an Irish pub. Louisa shows us her pictures as runner-up, sometime in the '60's, for Miss Magnolia, Houma, Louisiana. We indulge in chocolate walnut pie, more Winstons, pink napkins and spotlights over the table that look like candles. I buy a yellow baseball cap with blue wings for Nathan.

July 18

The world is full of still balloons and moths. They wander in and out of rooms, the neighbor's voices on a summer afternoon, late when your body is saturated with heat and your knees bend like a checkbook cover. The light quiets down and the wind stops. Even the crows are meek and stop their calls. Our heads are like a pile of cantaloupe. I'd like to take a meat cleaver and hack them to pulp, slice my kneecaps off to make them even.

July 19

The doors open a little and a butterfly who has beaten its wings in place flies out. He zooms and dips.

July 21

I can't remember whether I wrote to record my thoughts, or whether my thoughts are records of things I wrote.

She opens a letter from her sister and she sings.

August 6

Cutting the vines off at the trunk, death runs up a tree, across the tops of the elder and elm. Boats float behind pilings under the Tappan Zee Bridge and ducks nudge rocks for algae, their breakfast. Taking the kayaks, we herd a mother and four almost-grown babies back to our picnic under the trees.

Tom brings warm lemon chiffon pie onto the porch and slices it, like diving into a cool lake, cold and full of Tamarack trees and reflections of stars.

Gulls dip their tails up to water themselves and flies circle around the legs. In between those missing, the pilings lean and catch gull droppings in the sun.

On Maryo's back steps, we pour bottles of wine and beer, listen for the flickers and wait for a fight between two pileated woodpeckers before the sun goes down. We smoke all the cigars.

A flock of gulls sits in the middle of the tennis courts. Families light firecrackers from the beach.

August 9

We pull up weeds with Ruth. She is 87 and this is her idea. We listen to the hum of birds and motorcycles. Swimming to cool off in the early morning before the wind comes up, we have blueberry waffles. An egret flies overhead with his neck tucked in. I want to swim under his wings to see where he lands for the night.

August 10

The city is vacant and hot today. No flies. We have sleeping sickness from the heat, taking naps, struggling to get up at 10 so we can fix supper and pay attention to the evening. We make brownies and cold lemonade to have in bed, propped up on elbows and pillows to read.

August 11

Already you can't see across the Hudson. The morning air is white with haze, birds perch without noise in the trees. The boats sit in the river like an American painting. Kathy writes that she is holed up until September. The hotel is overrun with vagrants and music. She has no phone so I write: The world goes on out here, the subways hot with the smell of pee, an exceptional car air-conditioned in the middle of the morning. They are gutting the building next door, summer ganging up on us. We are in the space between our thoughts.

August 20

The crickets are six weeks away from the frost. They call to each other from either ear and I sit in the day, letting night slip by in their echoes. The house is my back. I breathe in the road and the milling weeds which bend to the asphalt before they can flower.

August 22

Stopping for fresh doughnuts and hot coffee on our way to a round of errands, Sunday is better. We get an earlier start, douse ourselves in sun. We have dinner in an old house and imagine snow lumping on the bushes outside. The kitchen help is listening to opera on the radio.

August 24

There is a tunnel through the joint diseases. Villagers walk around in warm-ups and capezios. Pulling on my heels I put on silk pants and feel like a dancer. In my dreams I run and leap; in daylight my feet won't lift or scatter, don't fly. A wrist alarm goes off as the lights go out.

August 25

Running under the trees the traffic is short and full of bakery and dump trucks, coffee steaming through gaps torn in the corner of plastic tops. A flock of purple martins makes a nervous path through the blowing fog, squeaking. As we climb through golden rod and chicory, one great white swan flies with slow wings and a fast heartbeat, taking over the lake, parting sky from sky.

We spend most of the evening with our imagination. No echoes. Gwen is still pregnant.

My grandfather picking over the canvas of hot air balloons, like monkeys picking over fur. His mother kept his report cards in the piano bench that sits at the edge of the bed, the cards long gone, the needlepoint worn like a carpet.

August 27

I walk up to the cookie machine. It's dark in Macy's basement and I try on gilt and silver walkers. We buy a quart of beer at the deli to drink to the new shoes.

September 1

The train runs across bridges built over the tops of water and we talk of suicide.

September 3

There is one new bird call this morning and no crows.

September 8

The gulls are flying north, geese in all directions, other birds are standing on the road after a day and night of rain. We relax after desert, Ravel and Poulenc.

September 9

The day has a high pitch like a large bird catching a draft under its wing feathers and gliding. There is a black-out below 14th Street and rows of New Yorkers walk out of subway tunnels avoiding the third rail. We head into the sun and walk around fat gas tanks, swapping histories and the stretch towards piecing our lives together when parents live in Los Angeles and children live in Cleveland, or die.

Pouring coffee onto the windowsill I watch it run over the edge onto the sidewalk, 13 stories below.

The city gets its teeth into the sky and pulls it overhead like a blanket. Trees yellow. Two kir, and the day has disappeared. The waiter lights the candles.

September 10

Weeds grow up around the last tomatoes and the sun moves south.

Letters in the form of cartoon animals walk off the page. There is a slit in your pants. We pick a green grasshopper off the pillow and toss him out the window. You paint your shoes white, iron your collar and I measure the buttons with my fingernail to replace them. I chew on thread and put my pins back in the shoebox, laying out projects in a row, hands resting on top of knees, thinking of the birds' densities when it rains. They have to shake the water from the tops of their shoulders.

September 11

The moon colors the horizon and pushes a map through trees. Bats squeak and a buck gives a hoarse call. It puts its hooves into the water and splashes the rocks.

Swimming back, the moon falls like a slow cloud and little bits of light catch in the leaves, like lightening bugs resting. Cars race by telephone poles. We stand to our shoulders next to the shore and watch as the moon sucks in the light. The edges sigh and break apart until my eyes focus. The last few yards I kick to get a good hold and stand balancing the water and the air. Before I turn I see the light from the moon just below the tops of the trees. It looks like a big town at night on the other side of the hills. We don't hear the buck until he makes a noise between a sneeze and a horse's snort. I am afraid that he'll go swimming and not know what to do when he meets us.

September 14

Sitting on the cement step outside the Laundromat with a bottle of sweating beer and tortilla chips reminds me of ten years ago, dried eucalyptus leaves outside the fence to the Greek Theatre. Lights and sounds from the street are disjointed as if I am in an all-night truck stop looking out.

September 16

There is a shape that beats in my head like a light and the hum on a train when it hits its peak and ceases to rattle.

September 17

I walk around the heat and Chevy van at Lloyd's Lumber stepping on a condom, already full and flattened out, cars driving over it after a Saturday night, the sound like the sound of a bicycle ride over the hot asphalt on the shoulder, at night, without the lights from cars, running over a plastic bag full of rainwater, but it is a raccoon, old and dead and bloated, picture of the car door opening a crack, peeling it off and dumping outside, the wind angling through the cemetery, the headstones, and depressions where the car tracks are.

September 27

Parallel to the sky I fly with the birds, the earth a head rest as we glide on the air drafts and suck in the sky until we are black silhouettes. The wind doesn't blow along the stone wall, and leaves, broken down from age and snow, piled at the bottom, the stream like the crackle of stepping on them and walking, the sound of the stream after five days of clouds and rain. Clouds and rain.